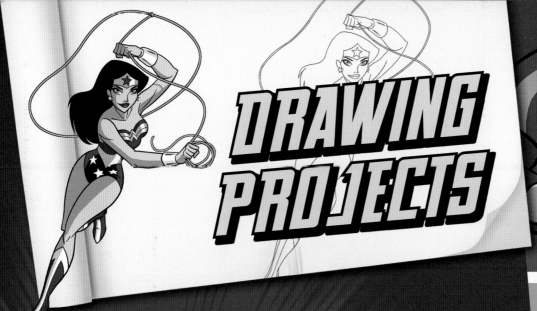

DRAWING PROJECTS

D0184922

LET'S DRAW AMAZING DC SUPER HEROES!

Superman and Batman aren't the only super heroes fighting the forces of evil. Wonder Woman, Green Lantern, The Flash, Supergirl and many other super heroes work just as hard to stop super-villains' wicked plans.

Super heroes come from a wide range of backgrounds and have many different powers. Some are human. Others come from alien worlds. Some heroes had loving families as children, while others grew up as orphans. Some were born with their abilities. Others got their powers accidentally or received them as gifts. However, as varied as their backgrounds are, super heroes all have one thing in common. They all have a strong desire to fight for justice and to protect innocent people.

Welcome to the world of DC Super Heroes! On the following pages you'll learn to draw Wonder Woman, Green Lantern, Cyborg and several other incredible heroes.

Use the power of your imagination to send your favourite super heroes on amazing new adventures!

WHAT YOU'LL NEED

You don't need superpowers to draw mighty heroes. But you'll need some basic tools. Gather the following stationery before starting your amazing art.

PAPER: You can get special drawing paper from art and craft shops. But any type of blank, unlined paper will be fine.

PENCILS: Drawings should be done in pencil first. Even professionals use them. If you make a mistake, it'll be easy to rub out and redraw. Keep plenty of these essential drawing tools on hand.

PENCIL SHARPENER: To make clean lines, you need to keep your pencils sharp. Get a good pencil sharpener. You'll use it a lot.

ERASERS: As you draw, you're bound to make mistakes. Erasers give artists the power to turn back time and rub out those mistakes. Get some high quality rubber or kneaded erasers. They'll last a lot longer than pencil erasers.

BLACK FELT-TIP PENS: When your drawing is ready, trace over the final lines with black felt-tip pen. The dark lines will help make your characters stand out on the page.

COLOURED PENCILS AND PENS: Ready to finish your masterpiece? Bring your characters to life and give them some colour with coloured pencils or pens.

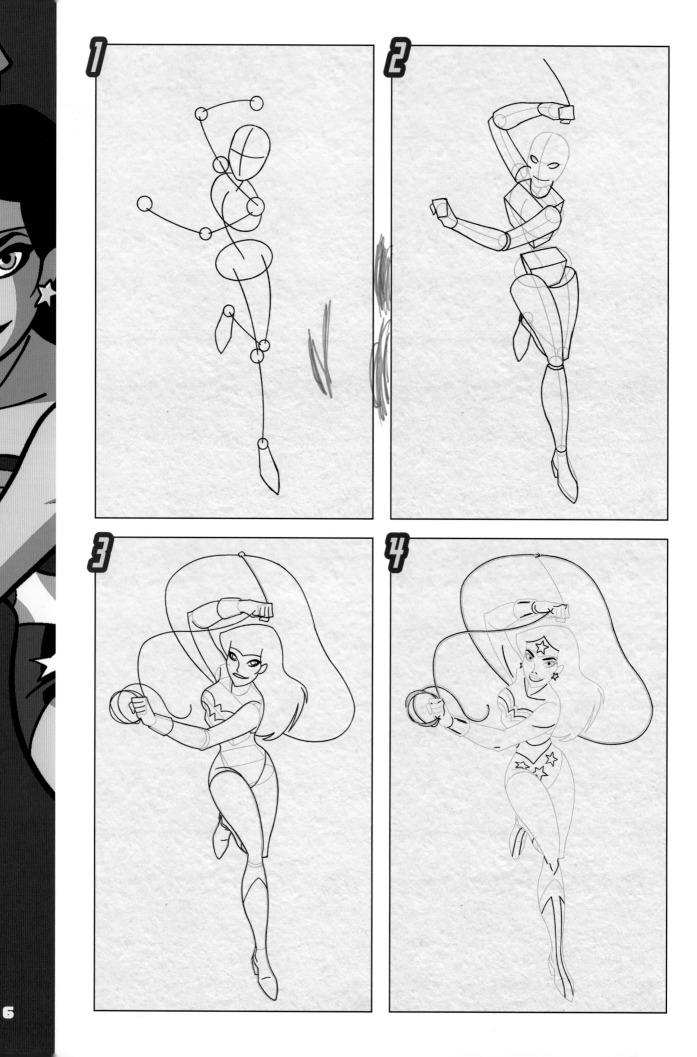

DRAWING IDEA
Try drawing Wonder Woman battling her arch-enemy Cheetah!

WONDER WOMAN

Real Name: Princess Diana

Home Base: Island of Themyscira

Occupation: Amazonian princess, crime fighter

Abilities: super-strength and speed, flight

Equipment: indestructible bracelets, magical tiara, Lasso of Truth

Background: Diana is the Princess of Themyscira, the hidden home of the Amazons. As she grew up, Diana knew she could be more than just an Amazonian princess. She trained hard and became highly skilled in hand-to-hand combat. Now, with her magical tiara, indestructible bracelets and Lasso of Truth, Diana fights the forces of evil as Wonder Woman.

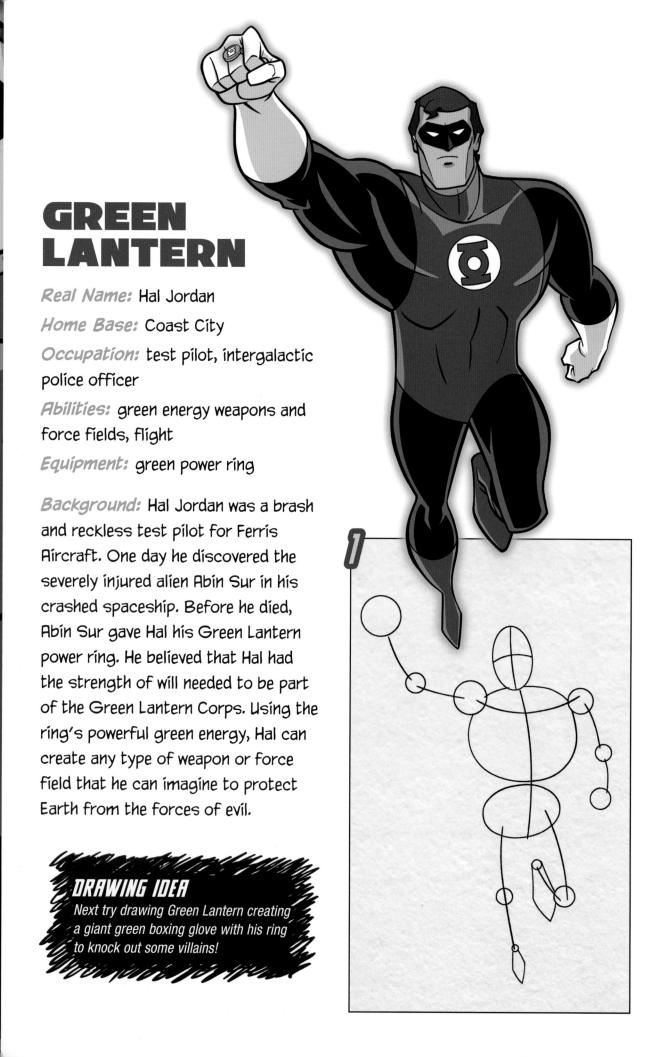

GREEN LANTERN

Real Name: Hal Jordan

Home Base: Coast City

Occupation: test pilot, intergalactic police officer

Abilities: green energy weapons and force fields, flight

Equipment: green power ring

Background: Hal Jordan was a brash and reckless test pilot for Ferris Aircraft. One day he discovered the severely injured alien Abin Sur in his crashed spaceship. Before he died, Abin Sur gave Hal his Green Lantern power ring. He believed that Hal had the strength of will needed to be part of the Green Lantern Corps. Using the ring's powerful green energy, Hal can create any type of weapon or force field that he can imagine to protect Earth from the forces of evil.

DRAWING IDEA
Next try drawing Green Lantern creating a giant green boxing glove with his ring to knock out some villains!

6

1

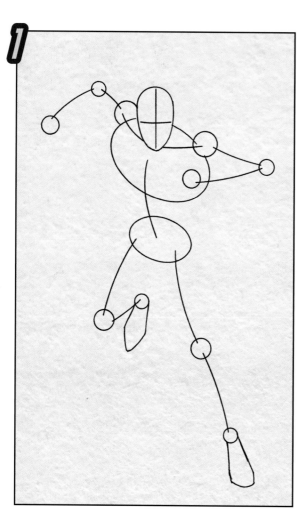

2

3

4

DRAWING IDEA
Try drawing The Flash
outrunning the icy rays
from Captain Cold's gun!

THE FLASH

Real Name: Barry Allen

Home Base: Central City

Occupation: forensic scientist, crime fighter

Abilities: super-speed, accelerated healing, phasing

Background: Forensic scientist Barry Allen was working in his lab one stormy night when a powerful bolt of lightning shot through a window. The lightning destroyed a chemical cabinet, soaking Barry in electrified chemicals. Shortly after the accident Barry discovered he could move at supersonic speeds. He can even vibrate his body so fast that he can phase right through solid walls! As The Flash, Barry uses his super-speed to save people from danger and to stop criminals in their tracks.

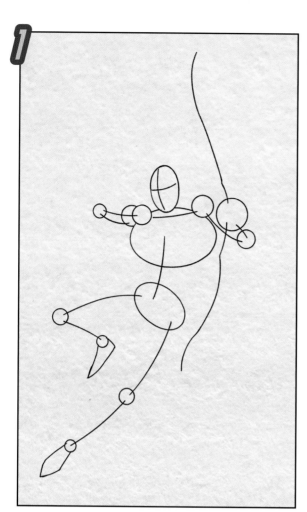

5

DRAWING IDEA
Next try drawing Green Arrow using his trick arrows to stop a criminal's getaway car!

GREEN ARROW

Real Name: Oliver "Ollie" Queen

Home Base: Star City

Occupation: billionaire businessman and politician, crime fighter

Abilities: expert marksmanship, hand-to-hand combat skills

Equipment: trick arrows

Background: As a boy, Oliver Queen was skilled with a bow, and his hero was Robin Hood. When Ollie's parents were killed, he grew into a rich and spoiled thrill-seeker who cared only for himself. But that all changed one day when he was stranded on a small island. There, he learned to survive by honing his fighting skills and becoming a master archer. After being rescued, Oliver decided to change his ways. He now models himself on his childhood hero. He dresses in green and uses his amazing archery skills to keep crime off the streets of Star City.

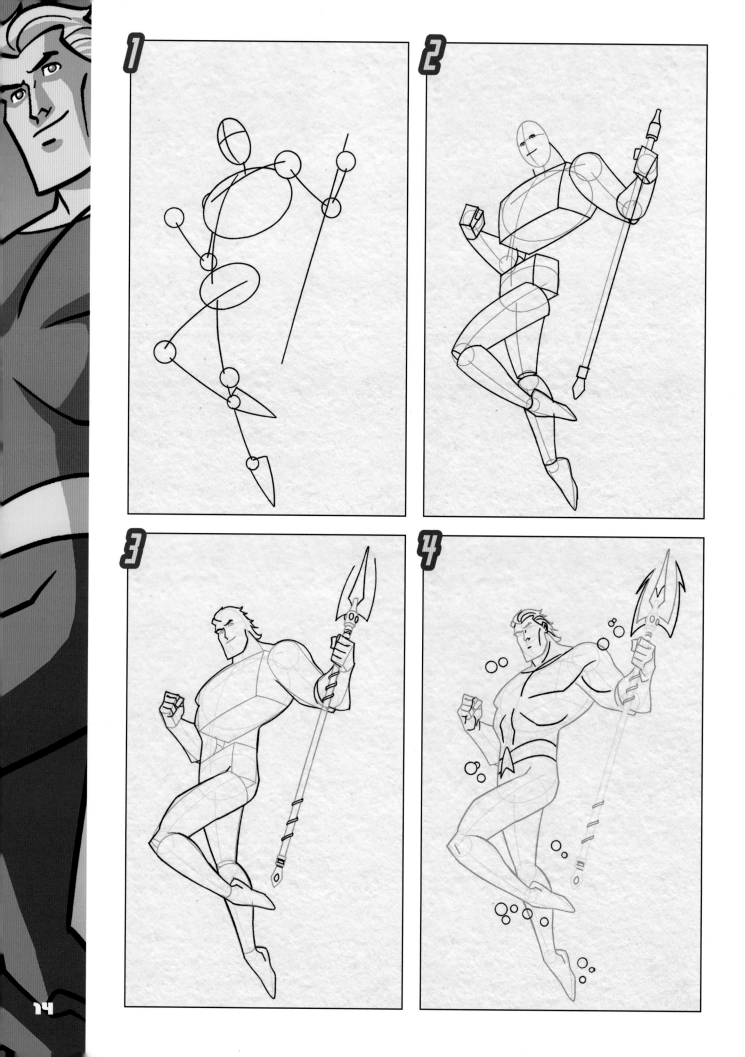

AQUAMAN

Real Name: Arthur Curry

Home Base: Atlantis

Occupation: King of Atlantis, protector of the oceans

Abilities: super-strength and speed, underwater breathing, telepathic communication

Background: Arthur Curry grew up as the son of a lighthouse keeper. At a young age, Arthur learned he could breathe under water and talk to fish and other sea creatures. Eventually Arthur learned that his mother was the Queen of Atlantis and that he would one day be a king. When he grew up, Arthur decided to use his powers to defend Earth's oceans and wildlife and help to stop the world's worst villains.

DRAWING IDEA
Next try drawing J'onn J'onzz taking the shape of a powerful animal to help Green Lantern defeat Sinestro!

MARTIAN MANHUNTER

Real Name: J'onn J'onzz

Home Base: Mars, Justice League Watchtower

Occupation: detective, Martian police officer

Abilities: super-strength and speed; flight; telepathy; shape-shifting; investigation skills

Background: When powerful aliens invaded Mars, the Martian race was nearly wiped out. As the last survivor, J'onn J'onzz managed to escape and fled to Earth. There he joined Earth's mightiest heroes to defeat the alien threat. Afterwards, J'onn decided to make Earth his new home. Using his shape-shifting ability, J'onn blends in with Earth's people. He uses his telepathic powers and detective skills to solve crimes and stop villains' wicked plans.

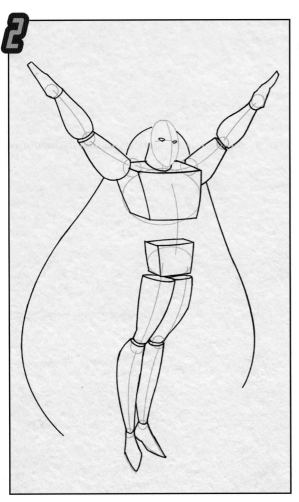

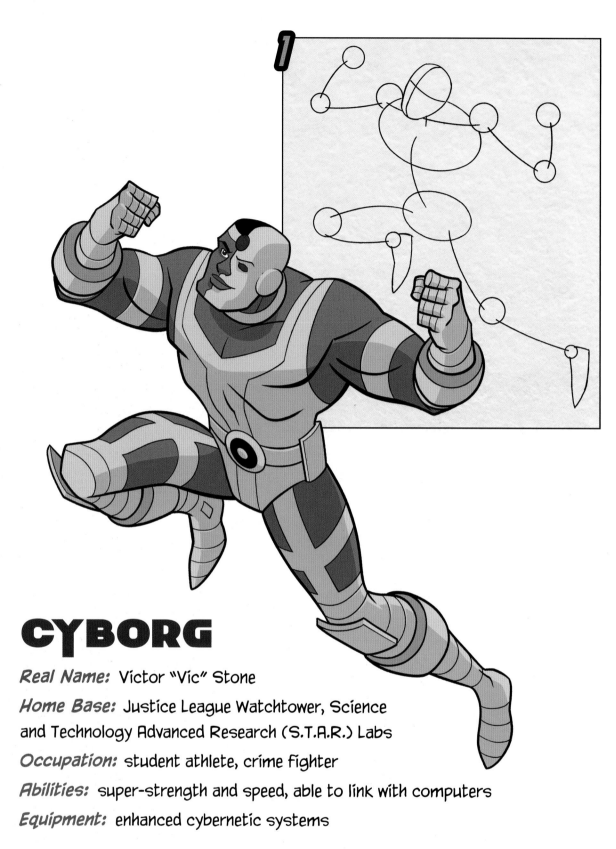

CYBORG

Real Name: Victor "Vic" Stone

Home Base: Justice League Watchtower, Science and Technology Advanced Research (S.T.A.R.) Labs

Occupation: student athlete, crime fighter

Abilities: super-strength and speed, able to link with computers

Equipment: enhanced cybernetic systems

Background: Victor "Vic" Stone was visiting his father at the local S.T.A.R. Lab when he was horribly injured in an accident. Vic's father saved his life by replacing much of his body with cybernetic parts. Vic's new body gives him superhuman abilities, and he can link with almost any computer in the world. Vic once dreamed of becoming a star athlete. But now he has a new purpose — to fight crime as one of the world's greatest heroes.

1

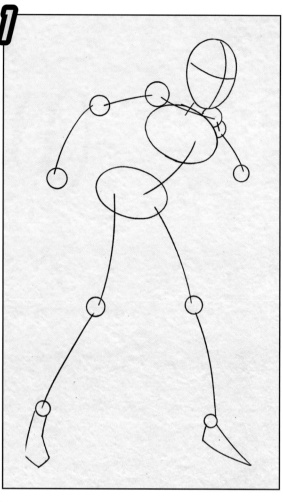

DRAWING IDEA
Next draw Black Canary using her special ability to help Green Arrow stop a bank robbery!

BLACK CANARY

Real Name: Dinah Lance

Home Base: Gotham City

Occupation: adventurer, crime fighter

Abilities: martial arts expert, ultrasonic "Canary Cry" scream

Background: Dinah Lance comes from a family of crime fighters. Her father is a police officer, and her mother fought crime as the original Black Canary. Her mother didn't want her to become a crime fighter, but Dinah followed in her mother's footsteps anyway. However, Dinah has a special ability of her own. Her ultrasonic "Canary Cry" scream can stun foes, damage objects and even shatter metal!

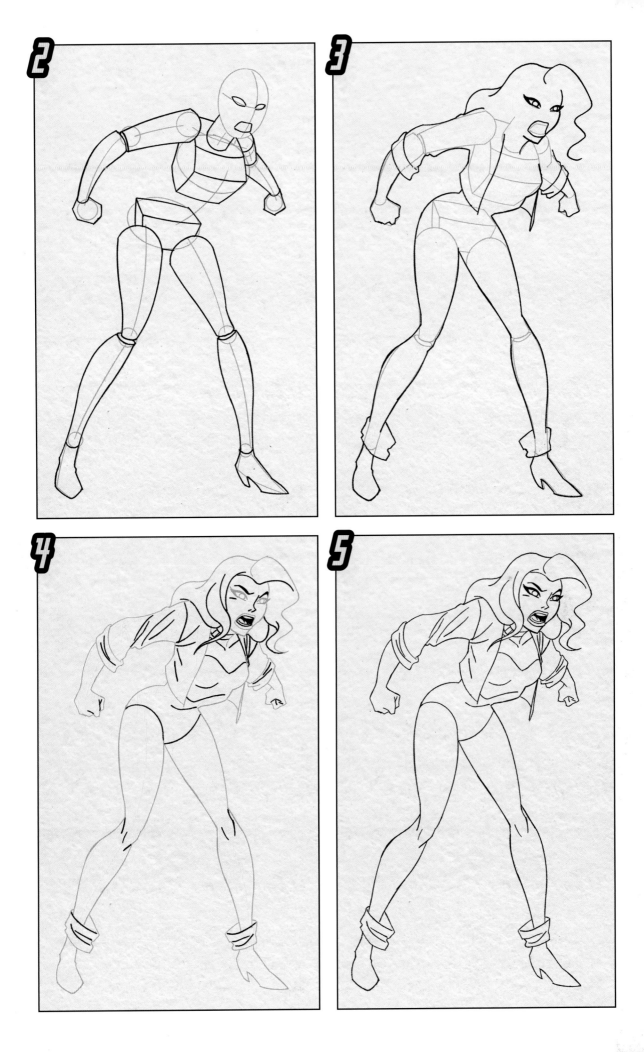

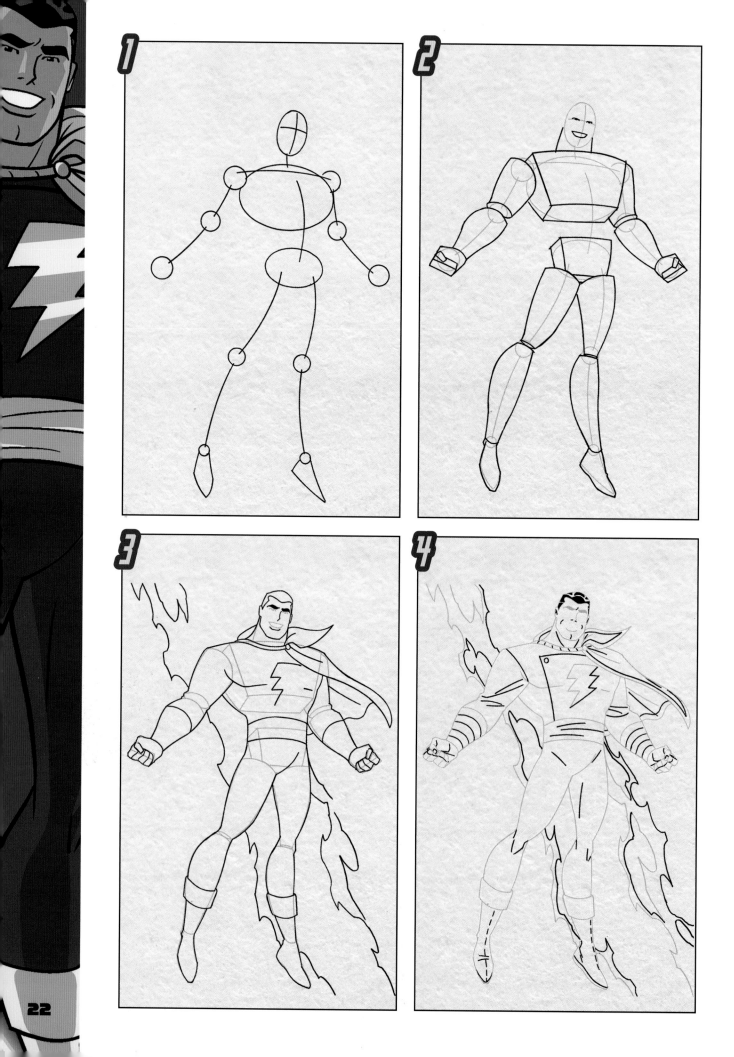

SHAZAM!

Real Name: William "Billy" Batson

Home Base: Fawcett City

Occupation: student, reporter, super hero

Abilities: super-strength, speed and stamina; flight; invulnerability

Background: Young Billy Batson's parents were killed during an archaeological expedition to Egypt. The powerful wizard Shazam soon learned about Billy and his strong sense of justice. The wizard gave Billy the powers of several historical figures. These included: the wisdom of Solomon, the strength of Hercules, the stamina of Atlas, the power of Zeus, the courage of Achilles and the speed of Mercury. Now, when Billy calls out the magic word "SHAZAM!," he is transformed into a mighty hero who is almost as powerful as Superman!

DRAWING IDEA
Try drawing SHAZAM! fighting his arch-enemy Black Adam to stop him from taking over the world!

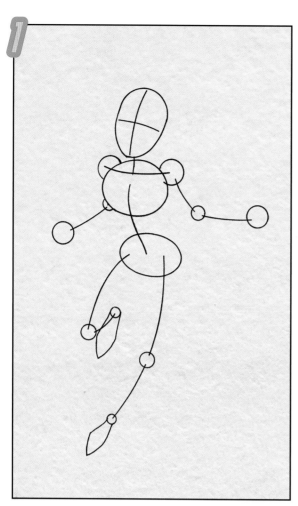

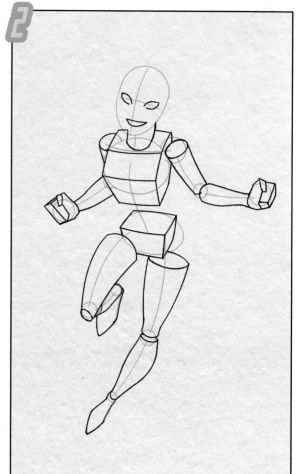

DRAWING IDEA
Try drawing Supergirl fighting alongside Superman to stop Brainiac from destroying Earth!

SUPERGIRL

Real Name: Kara Zor-El

Home Base: Metropolis

Occupation: student, super hero

Abilities: super-strength, speed and hearing; X-ray vision; heat vision; flight; invulnerability

Background: Kara Zor-El is Superman's cousin and the last survivor of Krypton's Argo City. Like Kal-El, Kara was sent to Earth in a spacecraft. Superman took Kara to live with the Kents as their teenage niece. The Kents taught her the same values they had taught Clark. Meanwhile, Superman taught her how to control her new-found abilities. Eventually Kara moved to Metropolis to fight crime as Supergirl.

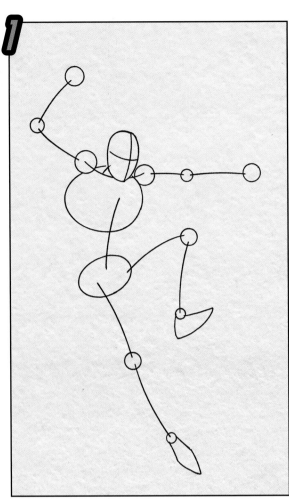

DRAWING IDEA
Now try drawing Nightwing using his acrobatic skills to take on a group of thugs on the street!

NIGHTWING

Real Name: Dick Grayson

Home Base: Blüdhaven

Occupation: adventurer, crime fighter

Abilities: master of martial arts and acrobatics, master detective

Equipment: pair of fighting sticks

Background: As a boy, Dick Grayson was a member of the Flying Graysons: a family of circus acrobats. When Dick's parents were killed in a tragic accident, Bruce Wayne took in the heartbroken boy. When Dick learned that Bruce was secretly also Batman, he began training to become the first Robin. Batman and Robin spent several years fighting crime together as the Dynamic Duo. But when Dick grew up, he struck out on his own. He created a new suit for himself and moved to a new city. Now he protects the streets of Blüdhaven as the acrobatic crime fighter, Nightwing.

THE JUSTICE LEAGUE

When Earth was invaded by powerful aliens, even the world's mightiest heroes were unable to defeat them on their own. Only by joining together did they have the strength to overcome the alien threat. After stopping the invasion, Superman, Batman, Wonder Woman, Green Lantern, The Flash and Martian Manhunter formed the Justice League. The heroes then built the Watchtower, a space station that orbits Earth. From here, the Justice League can watch over Earth and launch powerful defences to protect its people.

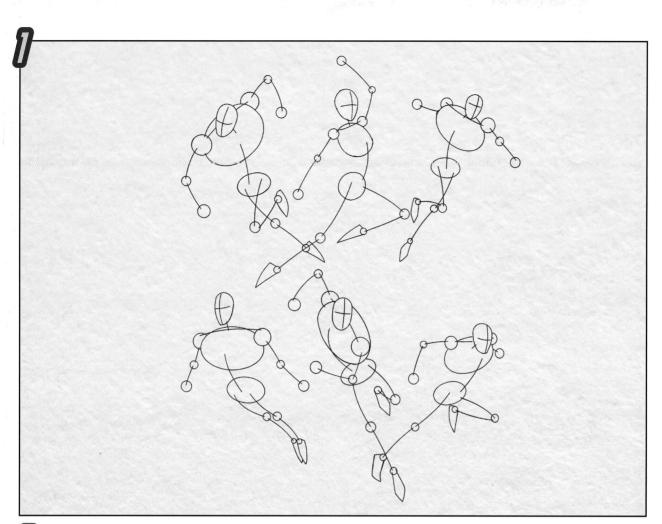

3

4

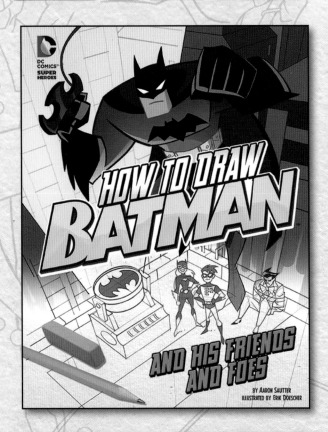

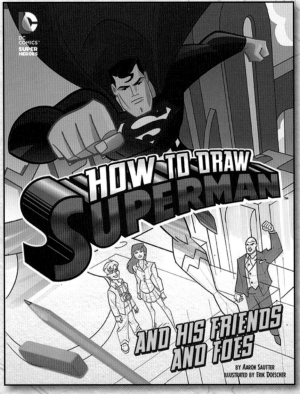

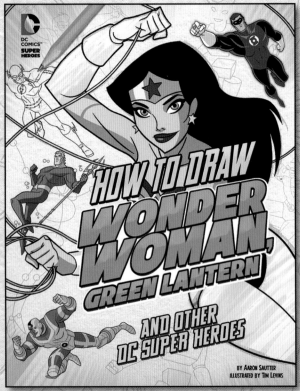